Winning Your Personal Injury Case

By

Doug Zanes, Attorney at Law

Disclaimer

Doug Zanes is licensed to practice law in the state of Arizona only. Neither Mr. Zanes nor Zanes Law guarantees that someone will win their case by following the steps outlined in this book. Case results are fact-specific to each case and the prior results that Doug Zanes or Zanes Law obtained for clients in no way reflects upon or is indicative of the results that you may be able to obtain on your own legal case by reading this book. Doug Zanes and Zanes Law strongly recommend that you consult with a qualified attorney in your state regarding any personal legal issue.

Table of Contents

CHAPTER ONE

Why Me?

In the seventeen years that I have been practicing law, I have heard this phrase more times than I can count. Imagine that you are going about your day, minding your own business, when, suddenly and unexpectedly, you get hurt. It's bad enough if this happens and it is your fault because, after all, accidents can happen and we can be at fault for them. But it's even worse if it is someone else's fault and you are innocent. In this case, you must deal with the life changing impact of another person's negligence. I say, "life changing" because just about every injury I have seen has been life changing, even if it was only life altering on a temporary basis because my client eventually recovered. But, nonetheless, it was "life changing."

So, why you?

Logically, we all know that there is no rhyme or reason as to why you were the one to get hurt. My clients generally chalk it up to bad timing and being in the wrong place at the wrong time. In the end, however, why you were the one who got hurt is much less important than ***how can you get back to*** *where you had been before the accident.* This "how" is what this book is going to focus on. We can't turn back time and change the past, but we can create a positive future, and knowing the "how" is the key to this.

Who am I?

Why should you trust me to show you the "how"? As you are aware from the cover of this book, my name is Doug Zanes. I am a trial lawyer. I am also the owner of Zanes Law, a law firm that solely represents clients who have been injured in accidents — all kinds of accidents. I have been practicing law for seventeen years and have represented thousands of injured clients. We have offices in both Tucson and Phoenix, Arizona, and our firm's mission is to expertly place our clients under our care, guidance, and protection for their maximum benefit. This is what my team and I do all day, everyday. I am a member of the Million Dollar Advocates Forum, one of the most prestigious groups of trial lawyers in the United States. Membership in the Million Dollar Advocates Forum is limited to trial lawyers who have won million dollar verdicts and settlements. Less than 1% of all U.S. lawyers are members.

In this book, I will share my many experiences in legal cases and with insurance carriers. By sharing my experience and expertise, it is my hope that you will find yourself in the best possible position to find a positive resolution to the awful situation you have found yourself in. If you find that you have questions that this book does not fully answer, please feel free to contact me directly at dzanes@zaneslaw.com and I will be more than happy to answer your questions and provide you with my input.

CHAPTER TWO

When the Injured Get Cheated

Protect Yourself from being a Two-Time victim!

Many people who are injured in a car accident actually get victimized a second time because the at-fault driver does not have enough insurance to fully compensate them. At Zanes Law, we have seen this happen with astonishing regularity. We regularly represent clients who are hurt because of another person's negligence. To make matters worse, we find out that the negligent person either had no insurance at all or he did not have enough insurance to completely compensate our client. This is where the injured victim gets the shaft. And, unfortunately, once an accident happens, it is too late to buy the insurance coverage that will protect you from this scenario. Long before an accident happens, we all have an opportunity to prevent further injury due to someone else's lack of adequate (or any) insurance.

In this chapter, I will discuss auto insurance coverage so that you will understand what you must do to protect yourself. That's right — protect yourself. You must do this for yourself, because despite the caring and clever television commercials that insurance companies put out, they really aren't in business to protect you against the bad things that can happen. They are simply in business to sell you an insurance contract that they hope they will never have to pay out on. To protect yourself, you need to know about — and purchase — the right type and amount of insurance.

How Much Coverage Do I Need?

Let's start with this question: "How much car insurance do I need?" I am surprised at how **few** times I have been asked this question. I don't think that many people give enough thought about the purpose of their car insurance or about how much car insurance they need. Indeed, before I began representing victims of car accidents, I certainly didn't give my car insurance coverage a second thought. I simply kept buying what I had always bought. Without proper knowledge, I figured it was enough insurance and the correct type of insurance. I was incorrect. Therefore, I am going to start by discussing liability car insurance coverage.

Liability car insurance coverage is the part of your car insurance that will pay someone who gets hurt if you cause an accident. If you run a red light and hurt someone, it certainly wasn't your intention. That's why it's called (and is) an accident, and accidents do happen. This coverage protects you from having to pay with your own money if you accidentally hurt someone. For example, your car insurance carrier pays the person hurt by the accident that you caused so that they are reimbursed for their medical bills, lost wages, and so that they are compensated for the pain, suffering, and inconvenience of being injured. Your insurance will pay them for any other losses that occurred because of this accident. If your insurance decides to fight the person that you hurt and you are sued, your insurance company will provide and pay the attorney who will defend you in this lawsuit. In addition, if you lose the lawsuit, they will then pay the judgment.

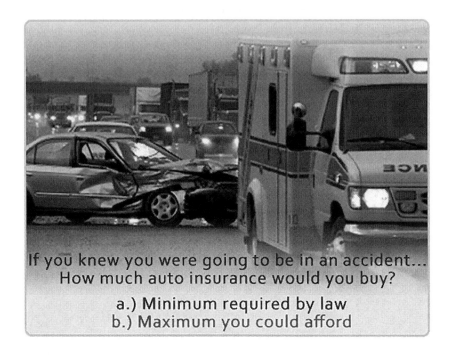

If you knew you were going to be in an accident...
How much auto insurance would you buy?
a.) Minimum required by law
b.) Maximum you could afford

Currently, every state has it's own laws which control the **minimum amount** of liability coverage that a driver must have. In Arizona, the law states that you **must** have a minimum of $15,000 in liability insurance coverage. However, we all know that this isn't nearly enough! In the event that you accidentally hurt someone, his or her medical bills alone could far exceed $15,000. If you are responsible for the medical bills, lost wages, pain and suffering, and potentially other damages, $15,000 doesn't do much to protect you!

In most cases, how much car insurance you purchase is directly proportionate to what you can afford. But, because of what I've discussed above, my recommendation is that everyone carry, **at the very least, $50,000 worth of liability coverage**. This will insure that anyone hurt by you in a car accident has a better chance of being fully compensated for his or her injuries. And, just as importantly, it will give you better protection against a personal liability suit. Remember, if you accidentally hurt someone so severely that your liability insurance policy limit isn't enough to completely compensate the person who is hurt, you could now be personally responsible for these costs. This means that you would have to pay the person the difference between the insurance money available and the actual value of his claim. Because of that, a person who earns a high wage and/or has a lot of assets needs significantly more car insurance coverage in order to be protected from personal liability. Although how much liability car insurance you buy is a personal decision, it is a decision that deserves some careful consideration.

Uninsured Motorist insurance coverage is the part of your car insurance that will pay **you** if you are hurt in a car accident and the at-fault driver does not have any car insurance. Unfortunately, at Zanes Law we see these kinds of uninsured car accidents almost every day — it is more common than people think. Look at it from this perspective: If someone is having trouble paying all of their bills, they usually don't stop driving or give up their car. In addition, they tend to choose to pay for groceries and rent before paying for their car insurance. So they let their car insurance lapse. If you are unfortunate enough to be hit by this person after their insurance policy has lapsed, an uninsured motorist has hit you. This means they will not have an insurance policy to compensate you for your injuries, missed time from work, pain and suffering, etc. If you find yourself in this situation, legally you can still sue the person that hit you and get a judgment, but, in my experience, the odds of you ever collecting money from this person are slim to non-existent.

For the above reason, it's my opinion that you MUST purchase uninsured motorist coverage when you purchase your liability insurance. Unlike your liability coverage, which exists to protect others, your uninsured motorists coverage exists to protect you and your family. Although I can't definitively prove it, I have always gotten the impression that insurance companies prefer to **not sell you uninsured motorists coverage**. This is because the actual premium piece of this coverage is extremely inexpensive for you, but it costs the insurance company a great deal of money because they end up paying out on this coverage over and over. Why? Insurance companies pay out on uninsured motorists coverage so often because there are so many uninsured drivers on the road. Therefore, I strongly advise you to purchase as much uninsured motorists insurance coverage as you can afford. Many years ago, I made this same decision because of what I see every day. Therefore, I purchase my car insurance in order to protect my family first and foremost.

Underinsured Motorist insurance coverage is the part of your car insurance that will pay **you** if you are hurt in a car accident by another driver who has liability insurance coverage, but does not have enough insurance to fully compensate you for your injuries and damages that you have incurred. Once again, at Zanes Law we regularly see clients who are hurt by a driver who may be insured but does not have enough insurance coverage to adequately compensate our clients. This is where underinsured motorists coverage comes into play. If you are unfortunate enough to be hit by a person who has low insurance policy limits, you risk not being fully compensated for your injuries **if you aren't carrying underinsured motorists coverage** on your car insurance policy. You can use your underinsured motorists policy to completely take care of your medical bills and to compensate you for your injuries, missed time from work, pain and suffering, etc.

For the above reason, it is also my opinion that you MUST purchase underinsured motorist coverage when you purchase your liability insurance and your uninsured motorists coverage. Similar to your uninsured motorists coverage, underinsured motorists coverage exists to protect you and your family, and is relatively inexpensive coverage to purchase. On many insurance policies it may simply be an additional $10.00 to $15.00 for six months worth of coverage. Based on my experience, I can guarantee that if you are hurt in an accident and it's not your fault, you will be very glad that you have it.

Although the above is not an exhaustive explanation of all the different insurance coverage available under an auto insurance policy, these are the three basics that will protect you. When speaking with your insurance company you should also consider purchasing **medical payments coverage**, property damage coverage known as **comprehensive/collision coverage**, and any other coverage that is available to you. Keep in mind that all states are different and have different laws regarding the legally required insurance coverage that a driver must carry. Because of that, the above information is simply general information. Please make sure that you research and understand your specific state laws in relation to auto insurance coverage.

So, there it is! To recap: In order to protect yourself, you must personally carry

1. Liability coverage of at least $50,000

2. Uninsured motorists coverage (UM)

3. Underinsured motorists coverage (UIM)

Remember, the UM and UIM coverage will provide you with the money that you need when the at-fault party does not have enough insurance to do that.

Be proactive and protect yourself and your family.

CHAPTER THREE

I Just Got Slammed!
What Should I Do Next?

Most of my clients are amazed at how quickly an accident actually happens. In an instant, it is over. Now what?

Be Proactive! An Accident Checklist:

After an accident, you want make sure you get as much information as possible. Sometimes this is easy because police will come to the accident scene and document everything, but you can't always count on this. For example, a few years ago, the police department in the City of Tucson decided that its police officers would no longer respond to normal, everyday car accidents. Their policy was (and still is) that they would only respond to an auto accident if someone were significantly injured or if the vehicles were blocking traffic. So, even if you are hurt but don't need immediate medical attention, you will be told by the police department to simply exchange information with the other driver. Therefore, after an accident you must to be proactive and get all the information that you may need. The following paragraphs will explain, in detail, why you should always do these four things after an accident: 1. Take photographs; 2. Get witness contact information; 3. Get other driver information, including insurance and personal contact information; and 4. Get medical attention if you have been injured.

Take Photographs

First, take photographs of everything that will be important later on. Take photos of all the cars involved in the accident. Get photos of the vehicles before they are moved off of the road. This can be very helpful in proving that the accident happened in the way that you say it happened. Often, the other driver has a different version of the accident and that version may place more blame on you.

You should also take photos of the physical damage to all of the cars involved. This will help in proving the significance of the accident's impact. This can be extremely important in an accident claim.

Document Visible Injuries

In addition, make sure that you take photos of any visible injuries that you have sustained. This can include bruising, cuts, scrapes, swelling, etc. Once again, this is important and can be extremely persuasive long after the accident occurred. For instance, when you are trying to explain to an insurance adjuster, arbitrator, or jury exactly how injured you were, pictures can truly be worth a thousand words.

Witnesses

Next, make sure that you get all the contact information for any person who saw the accident. This is a must! At Zanes Law, we have seen cases where the insurance company fights us on liability and blames our client for the accident. At that point, we need the independent witness. Unfortunately, if our client failed to get witness contact information at the scene of the accident, we have no way of finding him or her. Sometimes they just don't think of it, but other times our client thought that the police officer would get it, but he did not. This can be the difference between winning and losing your claim, so do not make this mistake. If you speak with a witness who saw the accident, get his name, address, phone number, and email address, if he has one. Make sure that you can find your witnesses when you need them later!

Other Driver's Information

Also, make sure you have all of the at-fault driver's contact information as well as their car insurance information. Unfortunately, I have been in a few accidents in my lifetime and I will tell you exactly what I did. First, I gave my insurance card to the other driver (even though I was not at-fault) and I also asked the other driver to give me his insurance card. This is simply easier because the insurance card has ALL of the insurance information, which includes the insurance company name, the policy number, the insured vehicle information as well as the information for the insured. Next, I insisted on seeing the other driver's photo ID. This way I could see their picture and also make sure that I had their real name, address, date of birth, and other identifying information. This is extremely important! I have seen far too many clients who were lied to and given false or incorrect information after they were involved in an accident. When that happens, it becomes extremely difficult to find an insurance company to make a claim against. In addition, when you sue another driver, you must have that driver's address in order to serve your lawsuit. In my experience as a lawyer, I have had many clients fail to get a driver's address. In these cases, serving a lawsuit becomes more expensive and more difficult. Again, do not simply get a phone number and a name. That's not nearly enough information. Insist on seeing photo identification and then copy that information.

Here is a real case example that we have seen more than once. Our client is involved in a car accident. The police do not come out to document the accident. The client does not take any photos, does not get any witness information, and only gets the name and phone number for the at-fault driver. Unfortunately, the other driver will not answer his phone and will not return our clients' calls when he tries to obtain the insurance information. The client then hires us because he has no idea what to do next. Unfortunately, we generally end up having the same problem and are unable to get the at-fault driver to speak with us and provide us with his insurance information. If our client has uninsured motorists (UM) coverage we will end up making the claim there, but if our client does not have UM coverage there isn't much we can do to help him. The moral of the story is this:

Get the complete information for the at-fault driver and his insurance company at the accident scene **before** he has time to think about how to get out of taking responsibility for the accident.

If there are Serious Injuries — Call 911 for EMS

Finally, if you have been injured you need to seek medical attention. If your injuries are significant and you need an ambulance, make sure that you dial 911 and get the immediate assistance that you need. If you don't need an ambulance, but believe that you need to go to an emergency room, please **do not hesitate** to go at any time after leaving the accident scene. In the next chapter, we will discuss medical treatment options in greater detail.

CHAPTER FOUR

I Feel Like I Got Hit by a Truck!

Seeking Medical Attention and Overcoming Obstacles

At Zanes Law we generally see two types of injury cases.

- First, we have cases where our client has obvious, severe injuries. That client is typically taken from the accident scene in an ambulance and is then hospitalized for various injuries such as broken bones or internal bleeding, and then typically requires surgery and/or hospitalization.

- Second, we have cases where our client has suffered soft-tissue injuries. Soft-tissue injuries consist of strained or sprained muscles, tendons, and ligaments. It is typically much harder to prove that soft-tissue injuries were actually caused by the accident than the severe injuries, but, in either case, the medical treatment that you receive is an extremely important part of your personal injury claim.

It is really very simple. Without medical care that documents and supports your injury claim, you have no injury claim. At least not an injury claim with much value. This is because without the medical care and its corresponding documentation, the insurance company will take the position that you were not hurt in the accident and should not be compensated because you were not hurt.

What do I do if I have no health insurance?

One challenge faced by many of our clients is a lack of personal health insurance. Without health insurance it can be extremely difficult to obtain medical care. Over the years at Zanes Law, we have built relationships with medical providers and are able to get our clients the medical care that they need even though they do not have health insurance. It is my opinion (and it is an experienced-based opinion), that if you are injured in an accident and you do not have health insurance, you should definitely hire an experienced personal injury trial lawyer to help you.

An experienced attorney can help you obtain the medical care you need and should be able to arrange payment for your care out of your injury case. Keep in mind, medical care is expensive and you need to make sure that it is paid for out of your injury case. You do not want to incur medical expenses only to learn later that there is no money to pay those bills.

Seek Medical Attention

I recommend that anyone who is injured in an accident to first go and see a medical doctor. I believe that, initially, the best medical doctor to visit is your primary care physician. You will need to tell your PCP about your accident and about every pain — from head to toe — that you are currently experiencing because of the accident. In my experience, your PCP will document every symptom and complaint. He will also be able to write you a prescription for medication (if you both believe it is needed) and he will be able to recommend what treatment you should undergo. I have seen PCPs refer clients to physical therapy, refer clients to more specialized medical doctors, and refer clients to chiropractors. I have also seen PCPs simply tell clients to go home and rest.

One thing to keep in mind is this: if your PCP simply tells you to go home and rest, and you do not feel better in a week or two, then you need to go back to your PCP for a follow-up appointment. Remember, your goal is to get better. Not to live silently in pain!

If you aren't better in a couple of weeks and you begin actively treating with chiropractic care, pain management, physical therapy, or some other type of medical care, it is extremely important that you do not miss your medical appointments. When you miss appointments and/or have gaps in treatment, the adverse insurance company will use that fact to argue that you weren't really hurt. Their position will be that if you are hurt and in pain you would go see the doctor and keep your appointments. It certainly seems logical, and insurance companies have found that juries agree with this argument. So, if you are hurt, make and keep your appointments and follow the recommendations made by your doctor!

Do You Need Long Term Care?

As clients move through their medical care, we typically see them end up in either one of two places. Clients either get better and recover from their injuries or they continue to have problems — even though they have received most of the medical treatment that is available and appropriate. This latter client continues to live in pain and continues to have problems. If you are this type of client, it is extremely important that these continued problems are fully documented by your doctor. It is important that there is absolutely no question as to how you are currently feeling.

Your goal when it comes to your medical treatment is simple — or at least it should be. Your goal is not to build the best possible injury claim or to create the most valuable claim. Your goal is to simply get better and get back to how you were **before the accident happened**. Remember, your injury claim will eventually end and you will receive whatever compensation you ultimately receive, but you have to live with your injuries. Therefore, your goal should be to recover 100% and feel great. Your goal should be to return to normal. Generally, no one will tell you this, but there is **never** enough money in any injury case to make you glad that this happened. But, if you are at least able to recover and not be burdened in the future, you are more easily able to move forward in a happy, positive way.

CHAPTER FIVE

I Can See the Money Train!
How Do I Catch It?

Again, you must understand that there is nothing that I, or anyone else for that matter, will be able to do that will make you glad that you have been injured in an accident. In my 17 years of handling personal injury claims, I can honestly tell you that it's rare for an injury victim to get rich off of a car accident or injury claim. However, a good injury lawyer will get your medical bills paid and will get you fair compensation for being injured and for having to go through the experience of being in an accident.

Million dollar settlements are often tied to horrific, life changing injuries, and most of that money goes to pay past and future medical bills. So, the truth is that you are much better off with a fair personal injury settlement and a complete medical recovery than you ever would be with a big settlement and the permanent, life-altering injuries that accompany that kind of accident.

In general, you are ready to attempt to settle your injury claim when you are either done with your medical care and have completely recovered or have recovered as much as you are going to recover. The actual value of your personal injury claim can be complicated to determine. Because of that, I am not going to attempt to address injury case valuation in great detail within this booklet. (I do intend to write another booklet that focuses solely on the ins and outs of case valuation, so keep an eye out for that.)

Medical Bills and Records

In order to attempt to settle your claim you will need to obtain complete copies of all of your medical records and bills from your medical providers. This sounds easy enough, but can sometimes present a challenge. The challenge lies in getting the insurance companies exactly what they want.

For example, some insurance companies want medical bills that actually contain the insurance codes that the medical insurance companies use to pay medical bills, but hospitals and doctors typically don't want to give individuals a copy of the bill that contains the coding.

In addition, the auto insurance adjuster will most likely want you to sign a medical release so that the adjuster can obtain his own copy of your medical records and bills. Because of these issues, my suggestion is that you sign the medical release for the adjuster so he can get his own copy, but insist that he send you a copy of everything that he receives. I also suggest that you personally obtain a copy of your medical records and bills from your providers so that you can compare what you receive to what the adjuster sends to you.

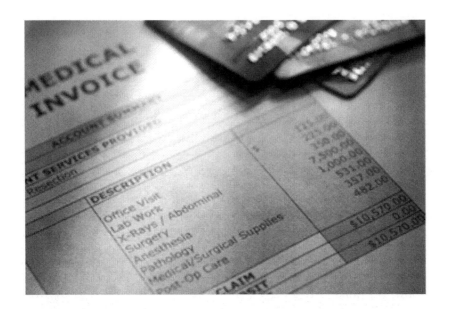

Once the adjuster has reviewed all of your medical bills and records, you are ready to attempt to settle your case. Reaching a settlement will require you to negotiate with the adjuster. As briefly discussed above, determining the value of your case can be complicated.

Over the years, an idea has caught hold that the value of a personal injury case is three times the medical bills incurred in the injury case. But this is far from an accurate valuation model. In fact, it is really a myth. Some cases are worth far less and some cases are worth far more, but the underlying measurement of case value is based on this question: "What will a jury award our client if we end up at trial?" As you can probably imagine, the answer to this question is based, in large part, on my experience as a trial lawyer and the experiences of the attorneys that I work with. Understandably, most individuals do not have this insight and experience.

Should I Handle My Own Claim?

Finally, if you decide to handle your own claim rather than hire a personal injury attorney, you need to know that you have lost your leverage with the insurance company. This is not always an issue that impacts what the insurance company is willing to pay, but it certainly can be. What does this mean? It's simple, in any injury claim your leverage is your ability to sue the at-fault party. In my experience, when an injured person does not have an attorney, the insurance company figures that they don't have to worry about their insured being sued. In addition, insurance companies know which attorneys are willing to sue on these cases and which attorneys aren't. So if you hire an attorney who has a reputation among insurance companies as an attorney who isn't willing to sue, you find yourself in the same situation as you would have been on your own, and you have to pay an attorney fee. Because of that, make sure you hire an attorney or law firm that is willing to litigate injury cases in order to get their clients a fair resolution. Because at this point your case either settles and is done or you will need to sue the person who hurt you.

CHAPTER SIX

"Dirty Tricks...

What the Business of Insurance is Really About"

When I first began representing injured clients 17 years ago, I asked myself this question: "Is the insurance adjuster my client's friend and advocate?" It took only one conversation with the very first adjuster I spoke with to find out the answer... NO!

People who have been injured forget that insurance is a business. Injured people believe that making a claim is about fairness, specifically about them being fairly compensated. Unfortunately, nothing can be further from the truth. *The insurance company's goal is to pay the least amount possible on your claim.* The less money they give you, the more money they have. It really is that simple. Add to the equation the fact that an insurance company has practically unlimited resources, decades of experience handling these claims in a way that is advantageous to them, and an army of lawyers, and you can see how the deck is stacked in favor of the insurance company.

Be Cautious Of An Early Settlement

Over the years I have come to the conclusion that, immediately after an accident, the goal of the insurance company for the at-fault driver is to resolve your injury claim quickly and for a small amount of money. In fact, some insurance companies advertise that they have a fleet of vehicles with adjusters who will come to the accident scene and help when you, their insured, is in an accident. I have been told by clients that these adjusters are most interested in issuing a check and getting a settlement release signed by the injured person who their insured hurt. Doesn't it make sense that an easy and cheap settlement is the real reason the adjuster came straight to the accident scene?

So why does this work? Why would someone settle right then and there? I believe that this works well for insurance companies because, immediately after many accidents, the victim doesn't feel hurt. Their adrenaline is pumping. They are thankful to not have broken bones and to not see any blood. So they take $500.00 or so and sign a liability release. Then, the next day, they wake up sore and only then realize that they are hurt, but it is too late because they have already settled their claim for pennies on the dollar. **Do not end up in that situation**. At Zanes Law, we have had client after client who initially thought that they were simply sore but would get better, only to learn later that they needed surgery to repair a torn up shoulder, a herniated disk in their back, or some other significant injury. These types of cases could be worth hundreds of thousands of dollars, not the mere hundreds that are offered initially after an accident. The moral of the story is this: Don't be victimized a second time by an early settlement!

I have also had clients come in to hire me and they have told me that they have cashed a check from the other driver's insurance company. The adjuster told my client that the check was only to reimburse them for their out-of-pocket expenses and lost wages, but <u>was not</u> the end of their case.

So, they took the check and cashed it. Then, when we contacted the insurance company, we were told that the client had already settled their case. When we reviewed the cashed check the case had, in fact, been settled. I was not a party to the conversation between my potential new client and the insurance adjuster, and I don't know exactly what was said, but I can tell you that I have seen this many times over my career.

People who have been injured also believe that in order to settle their case they must sign a settlement release. This, in fact, is not the case. If the client  is part of the settlement discussions and makes an informed decision to settle the case, it is probably settled. So, when you have accepted and cashed the insurance company's check, this is probably enough for the insurance company to win the argument that the case was actually settled. The best advice that I can give you is this: **Do not cash a check from an insurance company unless you are ready to settle your case or unless you are 100% sure that by cashing the check you are not settling your entire cas**e.

Typically, after an accident the insurance company for the other driver will want to get a recorded statement from you. They will ask you about the accident facts, your injuries, and anything else that they are interested in. Legally, you do not have to agree to give them this recorded statement. If you choose to, it's important that you understand the reason the insurance company is recording the conversation. They will use what you say against you in the future if, at some point in the future, you say something different.

For example, at Zanes Law we have had clients give a recorded statement prior to hiring us and before they actually felt injured. It was recorded that the client said that they did not believe that they were injured. Then, when the soreness set in over the next few hours and the client needed medical care, the insurance company used the fact that the client said they didn't believe that they were injured in order to deny paying for the client's care and to deny the client's injury claim.

Please, keep in mind that if you agree to give a recorded statement, you do not have the option to misspeak or to paint an incomplete picture. Doing so could hurt you in the long run.

CHAPTER SEVEN

"Don't Bill My Health Insurance,"
said the misguided patient!

Over the years, I have had clients who honestly believed that their health insurance should not have to pay for any of the medical treatment that they needed after being injured in an accident. Personally, I have never understood this perspective because this is why we have health insurance. We pay our health insurance premium every month so that if we ever become sick or hurt we are able to get the medical care that we need and also have it paid for. But, when some of us are hurt in an accident, we do not want to use our health insurance! I understand that many people want the at-fault driver who hurt us (and his auto insurance company) to be responsible for the payment of the medical bills. Of course, eventually they will be. But it's a process, and it can be a lengthy process. When you go to the hospital or a doctor, make sure you provide them with your insurance information and also make sure that you insist that they bill your health insurance for the treatment.

I have had clients tell me that while they were at the hospital, in the emergency room, the hospital realized the client had been in a car accident. At that point, the hospital staff actually told the client that they didn't need their health insurance information. The client was told that the hospital bill would get paid by the car insurance for the at-fault driver. This is a bad scenario for you, the patient, for a number of reasons. First, as the patient, you are personally responsible for this bill no matter what happens in your future car accident claim.

If, months later, it turns out that no car insurance exists that will pay this bill, you will then be personally responsible for it. Secondly, when this happens, it may now be too late for the hospital to send this bill to your health insurance company for payment. At this point, you will truly be personally responsible for your hospital bill. This can be extremely bad because a single outpatient emergency room visit can cost tens of thousands of dollars, and you would be responsible for the entire amount.

Here is an example of how, in my opinion, you should handle this situation. Let's say, for example, that you are in a car accident and are taken to the emergency room.  When you get to the emergency room and you fill out all of their paper work, you must make sure that you give them your complete health insurance information and that you give them your health insurance card to copy. Specifically tell them that you want them to bill your health insurance for the treatment that you are receiving. Then, after you are treated and sent home, you need to call the hospital billing department and make sure that they have all of your correct insurance information and you also need to make sure that they are billing your health insurance. Keep in mind that if your hospital bill is $10,000, your health insurance is probably not paying the hospital nearly that much money. Your health insurance will pay the hospital what they contractually have to pay the hospital per their agreement with the hospital. So, wouldn't you rather have this bill paid and taken care of by your health insurance? The alternative is that you personally are responsible for the full amount (not the lower amount that your health insurance would pay), and this is setting yourself up to be victimized once again. Please do not make this mistake.

CHAPTER EIGHT

The Three TRUTHS We Live By

I hope that this information has been helpful to you. It is meant to provide someone who has been hurt in an accident some basic information that will assist that person in handling their claim, or just in simply understanding some of the basic issues involved in an injury claim and the process. It is certainly not meant to be a comprehensive book that covers the many facets of all injury claims. It is **extremely important** that you understand that all personal injury claims are different and generally what must be done from a lawyer's perspective is based on the specific facts for that individual case. Unfortunately, the mistakes I see most injured victims make are directly related to the fact that they truly do not realize the complexity of most personal injury cases. They do not have the advantage of being involved in thousands of these cases both prior to litigation and after suing someone. I also see attorneys who only handle a handful of injury cases make these same mistakes. I'm sure you can understand that experience is key to getting the best possible resolution to your injury claim.

At Zanes Law we live by **3 TRUTHS** that are inherent to all personal injury cases, and I think anyone who has been injured must understand these truths. The following are the 3 TRUTHS you should know before either representing yourself on your injury claim or before hiring an injury lawyer to help you with your claim.

1. There is nothing that your injury attorney will be able to do that will make you glad that this has happened.

The truth is that in 17 years of handling personal injury claims I can honestly tell you that it's rare for an injury victim to get rich off of a car accident claim. However, a good lawyer will get your medical bills paid and will get you fair compensation for being injured and being subjected to the experience of being in a car accident. Please understand that a million dollar settlement is tied to horrific, life changing injuries, and most of that money goes to pay past and future medical bills. In the great majority of situations, you are much better off with a fair personal injury settlement and a complete medical recovery than you ever would be with a big settlement and the permanent, life-altering injuries that accompany a million dollar case.

2. It's true, you can settle your own car accident claim without the help of an attorney. But at what cost? In the long run it may end up costing you more in terms of time, aggravation, resources, and money. A good attorney will evaluate your car accident case and give you an opinion for free at an initial consultation. **The truth** is that most of the time a good personal injury attorney will help you get a better resolution to your claim than you would be able to get on your own, and you will save yourself much time and frustration by getting professional help.

3. You are the one who has been injured in the accident and your injury case is 100% about getting you compensated. **The truth** is that if we at Zanes Law believe that you are better off settling your injury case on your own, we will tell you. Why? We want you to have as much money as possible in your pocket at the

end of your car accident or personal injury claim. A good attorney will be honest with you and release you to finish your injury claim on your own if they believe that you will ultimately have a better case resolution without them. No strings attached.

After representing thousands of clients through the years, my team and I have learned that the above truths apply to most of our clients and to most of the cases that we work on. We know that if we live these truths every day we will do a better job at helping those who have been injured, and in the great, grand scheme of things, we, as a firm, will be rewarded for looking out for our clients. At Zanes Law we truly put our clients under our care, guidance, and protection, and you deserve nothing less!

INJURY LAWYERS

Central Tucson

3501 E Speedway Blvd #101

Tucson, Arizona 85716

Phone: 520.441.3720

South Tucson

1185 W Irvington Road #155

Tucson, Arizona 85714

Phone: 520.441.3867

Phoenix Law Office

4222 E. Thomas Rd, Ste. 230

Phoenix, Arizona 85018

Phone: 602.459.9678

Glendale Law Office

6601 W. Bethany Home Road, Ste. A10

Glendale, Arizona 85301

Phone: 623.552.5503

Made in the USA
San Bernardino, CA
18 February 2020